ISLAM
UNVEILED

Eleventh Edition

Abdullah al-Araby

THE PEN vs. THE SWORD
P.O. Box 661336
Los Angeles, CA 90066
USA.

This Book...

This book is an attempt to explore the fundamental teachings of Islam. However, we are not trying in this book to make a blanket statement about Muslims.

While many Muslims practice the teachings of Islam shown in this book, we realize that there are other Muslims who may have different interpretations, and thus do not follow these teachings to the letter.

Nothing in this book is written with the intention of offending anyone. Our objective is only to present the truth, with love and humility.

Quotations of the Quran used in this booklet are from: <u>The Noble Quran</u>; by Abdullah Yusuf Ali.
http://www.usc.edu/dept/msa/quran/

Quotations of the Hadith are from: <u>The translation of the meaning of Sahih Al-Bukhari</u>; Muhammad Muslim Khan, Kazi Publication, Lahore, 1979.

Quotations of the Bible are from: <u>The Holy Bible in the King James Version</u>; Thomas Nelson, Nashville, 1976.

First Edition:	November, 1987	Second Edition:	June, 1989
Third Edition:	October, 1992	Fourth Edition:	February, 1994
Fifth Edition:	August, 1995	Sixth Edition:	March, 1997
Seventh Edition:	August, 2000	Eighth Edition:	November, 2001
Ninth Edition:	January, 2002	Tenth Edition:	June, 2002
Eleventh Edition:	September, 2004		

ISBN 0-9656683-6-3

Printed in the United States of America

CONTENTS

Page

Foreword 5
Introduction: BEYOND THE FAÇADE 6

Chapter I: THE MESSENGER AND THE MESSAGE
1 - Mohammed 15
2 - Islam 16
3 - Jihad (Holy War) 17

Chapter II: THE ISSUES According to the Quran
1 - Women's rights 19
2 - Sex and marriage 21
3 - Human rights 22
4 - Democracy 25
5 - Eternal security 27

Chapter III: THE ISSUES According to the Hadith
1 - Women's rights 31
2 - Sex and marriage 32
3 - Human rights 33
4 - Eternal security 34
5 - Medicine 35
6 - Miscellaneous 35

Chapter IV: THE DIFFERENCE
1 - Christianity vs. Islam 37
2 - The Bible vs. the Quran 39
3 - God vs. Allah 46
4 - Jesus vs. Mohammed 52
5 - Jesus is the difference 57

Chapter V: IS ISLAM A LEGITIMATE EXTENSION OF
          CHRISTIANITY?
1 - Was Mohammed Prophesied in the Bible? 58
2 - Do Islam and Christianity agree on the basics? 59

Conclusion 64

"... and others were tortured, not accepting deliverance; that they might obtain a better resurrection."

Hebrews 11:35

Dedication

This book is dedicated to the memory of Hussein Sudmond in Iran, Naimat Ahmer in Pakistan, Abdel Hamid Bashary in Egypt, Sadek Abdel Karim in Saudi Arabia, Zia Nodrat in Afghanistan... and the many others, who chose to face imprisonment, torture and death, in their Islamic countries, rather than deny their faith in Jesus Christ.

This book is also dedicated to the memory of the thousands of innocent people who lost their lives in the brutal attacks by Muslim extremists, on September 11, 2001, in New York, Washington D.C. and Pennsylvania.

FOREWORD

Islam is being presented to the world today packaged in a fancy wrapper.

Muslim activists emphasize that Islam is the "true religion" that calls on followers to believe in Allah and in the last day, to enjoin what is just, to forbid what is evil, to observe prayers, and to practice charity (Surah 9:71). These basic tenets of Islamic teaching sound so right, so good, that they have drawn many naive people into the fold of Islam.

There is, however, another side to Islam usually hidden from prospective converts. Major issues of life that are part of Islam are carefully avoided, obscured or omitted from the call to faith. Some passages of the Quran are inaccurately translated from the original Arabic to lure converts.

The purpose of this book is to unwrap that attractive package and to explore what is inside. The aim is to expose some of the teachings of Islam that are withheld from seekers, and to help the reader gain a more realistic insight of what it is like to live under such teachings.

This study is by no means exhaustive; it gives a sampling only. Those who wish to investigate matters more thoroughly may write to us, asking for other resources.

My desire in writing these pages is that God, the Almighty, will lead us all in the way of truth and life everlasting.

Abdullah al-Araby

INTRODUCTION

BEYOND THE FAÇADE

The "Islam" that Muslim activists present to the West these days is completely different from the Islam we, who once lived in the Islamic world, have known and experienced. This is a new edition - revised, modified, expanded and abridged - of the real Islam. A major facelift operation has been taking place.

I must acknowledge, however, that the international Islamization movement, in recent years, has grown much in both intelligence and sophistication. They lacked power, so they decided to be smart. Since they could no longer use the sword to conquer the world, as they once did, they decided to use more subtle methods, taking advantage of democracy and freedom of expression in the West.

The following are some of the methods Muslim activists are now adopting in the West:

1 - CHANGE OF IDENTITY

Muslim activists in the West avoid referring to teachings that may offend the Western citizen. As an example, they never mention the Islamic code of punishment.

They stress that they believe in Moses and Jesus. They no longer call Jews and Christians infidels, nor would they call them "Zionists" or "Crusaders."

The last thing they want to do is to shock people. They have a Muslim host, with a Christian name, "Paul", on their TV program. Names like Mohammed, Mustafa and Omar were too strong to swallow, they thought. They use the term "Sunday School" in place of "Friday Class," and they end their speeches with the Christian expression "may God bless you."

They boast about being Americans, and have the American flag cover the background of their TV program set. This, at a time when Muslims are burning the American flag, in their daily rituals in Islamic countries around the globe, calling America "The great Satan."

2 - CHANGE OF VOCABULARY

They are now using a completely new terminology. Words like Love, Grace... are now part of their vocabulary. Theological Christian terms such as: Salvation, Justification and Sanctification, are now part of their teachings.

They change Quranic translations in order to hide some of Islam's harsh teachings. An example is the new French translation of the Quran. That translation has caused a tremendous furor among Muslim fundamentalists because it has attempted to please Jews by modifying some verses of the Quran that condemn Jews. One verse used to read, *"The people of Israel, after sowing corruption twice on earth for the purpose of dominating other peoples, will push themselves up into a position of extreme power before being punished by God."* The new translation reads just the opposite: *"The people of Israel will be twice destroyed as an innocent victim, and God will reward them by elevating them to great heights."*

3 - CHANGE OF STRATEGY

Instead of living in isolation from society, their new strategy lies in trying to be accepted, included, and involved in all activities whether they be religious, social, or political.

They are now becoming active in partisan functions in order to have a say in party platforms. They conduct letter campaigns to members of Congress to influence legislation. They run for public offices in hope of reaching a position of authority. They make full use of their voting power to get concessions in their favor. They try to be represented on educational committees for the purpose of changing educational programs to suit their beliefs.

The stage of weakness and the stage of Jihad (Holy War)

These new tactics we have discussed are not without precedent in Islamic history.

Mohammed Hassanein Heikal, the noted Egyptian author, refers to this concept in his book "Autumn Furor," page 285. He states: "So, the element of Jihad emerged in the ideology of Abul Aala Almaudoody. He went on to differentiate between two separate stages a Muslim community goes through:

"The stage of weakness - In it a Muslim community is unable to take charge of its own destiny. In this case - according to his thinking - it must withdraw for the purpose of preparing itself to be capable of executing the second stage.

"The second stage is the Jihad stage, and it will come when the Islamic community has completed its preparedness and is ready to come out of its hiding to take charge, through Jihad.

"In this, Abul Aala Almaudoody was making a comparison between the two stages of weakness and Jihad on the one hand, and on the other hand, Mohammed's struggle in Mecca, then in Medina."

Mohammed of Mecca and Mohammed of Medina

Historians agree that there is a big difference between Mohammed's personality in Mecca and his personality after his migration to Medina.

In Mecca, Mohammed was weak, struggling to be accepted, often mocked and ridiculed. He tried to appeal to the people of Mecca by being compassionate and loving. His teachings condemned violence, injustice, and neglect of the poor. However, after he moved to Medina and his followers grew in strength and number, he became a relentless warrior, intent on spreading his religion by the sword.

This change in Mohammed's personality becomes apparent by comparing the Meccan and Medinan Surahs (Chapters of the Quran). The following are some examples. Due to the unusual fashion in which the Quran was arranged, the number of a chapter and verse does not indicate a chronological order.

In Surah 73:10 **God tells Mohammed to be patient with his opponents,** *"Have patience with what they say, and leave them with noble (dignity)."* Later in Surah 2:191, **God orders him to kill his opponents,** *"Slay them wherever ye catch them and turn them out from where they have turned you out."*

In Surah 2:256 **God tells Mohammed not to impose Islam by force,** *"Let there be no compulsion in religion;"* while in verse 193 **God tells him to kill whoever rejects Islam,** *"Fight (Kill) them on until there is no tumult or oppression and there prevail justice and faith in Allah."*

In Surah 29:46 **God tells Mohammed to speak nicely to people of the Book (Christians and Jews),** *"And dispute ye not with the People of the Book except with means better (than mere disputation) unless it be with those of them who inflict wrong (and injury): but say "We believe in the Revelation which has come down to us and in that which came down to you; Our Allah and your Allah is one; and it is to Him we bow (in Islam)."* while in Surah 9:29 **God tells him to fight the People of the Book,** *"Fight those who believe not in Allah nor the last day...Nor acknowledge the religion of truth (Islam), (even if they are) of the people of the Book, until they pay Jizya (tribute tax) with willing submission, and feel themselves subdued."*

To justify this sudden change in the Quran's mood from peaceful to militant, conciliatory to confrontational, Mohammed claimed that it was God who ordered it. It was God who abrogated the peaceful verses and replaced them by harsh ones.

However, the truth of the matter, as Almaudoody puts it, is that Mohammed finally became strong enough to move from a stage of weakness to the stage of Jihad.

Today, in the West, we are witnessing the Islamic stage of weakness, but let's not be fooled, the stage of Jihad is coming, sooner or later. This meek little lamb will turn out to be a ravenous wolf, the sweet melodious "Baa Baa" will change to a thunderous roar.

The Peaceful Prophet of Mecca Changes Into The Ruthless Warrior of Medina

Mohammed's decision to relocate his new movement from Mecca to Medina presented an economic challenge. He had to find a method of supporting himself and his followers that would also provide an adequate base to finance the ever-increasing demands of the Muslim movement. The traditional method for acquiring wealth among the Arabs at the time was attacking other tribes and seizing their possessions. Muslims living in Medina found no easier way than doing that. They started to make raids (Ghaswa) on other tribes and passing caravans.

The first raid was called an-Nakhla. Muslims, led by Abdullah bin Jahsh, waited in ambush near a place called an-Nakhla and took the passing Qorayshite caravan by surprise. Muslims killed the leader of the caravan and captured two men and the entire cargo goods.

The turning point in Mohammed's life, however, was the raid against Badr. Muslims were able to kill dozens of Meccans and take scores of prisoners and much booty. On their way back to Medina some of those prisoners were put to death. One of them was a man named Uqbah bin abi Muait. Before his execution Uqbah pleaded with Mohammed saying, "Who, then, will take care of my little girl?" Mohammed answered, "Hell-fire."

After that, a confident Mohammed started moving against his

enemies in a series of attacks that resulted in the elimination of Jewish tribes and the assassination of certain individuals for the slightest offense. The assassination of Kaab ibn al-Ashraf, of the Jewish tribe Banu al-Nodair, was prompted by Kaab showing sympathy for the Qorayshites, and then when he returned to Mecca he recited amorous poetry to Muslim women. Mohammed was enraged and asked for volunteers to rid him of ibn al-Ashraf. Those who volunteered asked for permission to lie in order to lure him out of his house at night into a remote area where they were able to kill him.

A poetess named Asmaa bint Marwan was ordered to be killed for uttering a few verses of poetry criticizing Mohammed. A Muslim assassin, acting on Mohammed's orders, crept at night into the woman's bed while her suckling baby was attached to her breast. The man plucked the baby from her breast and then plunged his sword into her abdomen. Later, the killer, fearing the consequences of his crime, asked Mohammed, "Will there be any danger to me on her account?" Mohammed answered, "Two goats will not butt each other about her."

There were many other outrageous assassinations ordered by Mohammed. Abu Afak, an old man of 120 years of age was murdered for composing poetry critical of the Prophet. Another brutal assassination was against an aged woman by the name of Umm Kirfa. Muslims tied her legs to camels which were then driven in opposite directions. The poor woman was split into two pieces.

The reality of the Muslim assassin's brutality is punctuated by their practice of cutting off the heads of victims and bringing them to Mohammed. As the killers came into view carrying with them the evidence of Allah's victory over the enemies of Mohammed, a jubilant Mohammed would cry, "Allaho Akbar," (God is great)!

The list of these horrendous acts is too long, much is too repulsive to mention. What has been cited should be sufficient to say about the man that Muslims describe as the "prophet of peace and mercy"!

The essential problem is that the fruit of Mohammed's legacy exists today. As Muslims get deeper into Islam, they simply try to follow in the footsteps of their prime example. Can one still wonder why so much violence is committed, around the world, in the name of Islam?

The Abrogator and the Abrogated

In their attempt to polish Islam's image, Muslim activists usually quote the Meccan passages of the Quran that call for love, peace and patience. They deliberately hide the Medenan passages that call for killing, decapitating, and maiming.

Muslim activists also fail to reveal to people in the West a major doctrine in Islam called "al-Nasikh wal-Mansoukh" (the Abrogator and the Abrogated). This simply means that when a recent verse in the Quran gives a contradictory view to another verse that preceded it (chronologically), the recent verse abrogates (cancels and replaces) the old verse and renders it null and void.

This doctrine is based on the Quran, where Allah allegedly says in Surah 2:106, *"None of Our revelations do We abrogate or cause to be forgotten, but We substitute something better or similar: Knowest thou not that Allah Hath power over all things?"* Also, in Surah 16:101 *"When We substitute one revelation for another, and Allah knows best what He reveals (in stages), they say, "Thou art but a forger": but most of them understand not."*

One of Islam's classical reference books, written by a recognized Muslim scholar, deals in great detail with the subject. The title of the book is *"al-Nasikh wal-Mansoukh"* (The Abrogator and the Abrogated) by *Abil-Kasim Hibat-Allah Ibn-Salama Abi-Nasr.* The book goes through every chapter in the Quran and points in full detail to every verse that has been cancelled and what verse replaced it. The author noted that out of 114 Surahs (chapters) of the Quran, there are only 43 Surahs that were not affected by this concept.

An example of the abrogation: there are 124 verses that call for tolerance and patience which have been cancelled and replaced by this one single verse: *"Fight and slay the Pagans wherever ye find them, and seize them, beleaguer them, and lie in wait for them in every stratagem (of war)....."* **Surah 9:5**

One doesn't help but wonder: how Allah, the all-powerful, the all-knowing, needs to revise himself so often?

The <u>Real</u> Attitude of Islam Towards Christians and Jews

We have discussed the facade that Muslim activists in the West have been displaying to Christians and Jews. They have been saying that Islam is compatible with Christianity and Judaism. Some Christian and Jewish leaders have been deceived into believing them. The following "Fatwa" (Religious opinion) by a prominent Islamist tells, exactly and bluntly, what Muslims <u>really</u> think of Christians and Jews.

<u>From the Muslim site of Ibrahim Shafi on the Internet:</u>
http://www.wam.uwd.edu/~ibrahim
[Answer by Shaikh Ibn Uthaimin]

<u>Question:</u> One of the preachers in one of the mosques in Europe claimed that it is not allowed to consider Jews and Christians disbelievers. You know - may Allah preserve you - that most of the people who attend the mosques in Europe have very little knowledge. We fear that statements like this one will become widespread. Therefore, we request from you a complete and clear answer to this question.

<u>Answer:</u> I say: The statement that came from that man is misguidance. In fact, it can be blasphemy. This is because Allah has declared that Jews and Christians are disbelievers in His Book. Allah has said, *"The Jews call Uzair a son of Allah and the Christians call Christ the son of Allah. That is a saying from*

13

their mouths; (in this) they but imitate what the unbelievers of old used to say. Allah's curse be on them: how they are deluded away from the truth! They take their priests and their anchorites to be their lords in derogation of Allah and (they take as their Lord) Christ the son of Mary: Yet they were commanded to worship but one Allah: there is no god but He. Praise and glory to him: (far is He) from having the partners they associate (with him)." [Al-Taubah 9:30, 31]

That shows that they are polytheists who associate partners with Allah. In other verses, Allah has made it clear that they are disbelievers:

"In blasphemy indeed are they who say that Allah is the Christ, son of Mary." [Al-Maidah 5:17 and 72]

"They do blaspheme who say, 'God is one of three [in a Trinity]." [Al-Maidah 5:73]

"Curses were pronounced on those among the Children of Israel who rejected faith by the tongue of David and of Jesus the son of Mary." [Al-Maidah 5:78]

"Those who reject (truth) among the People of the Book and the Polytheists will be in hell-fire to dwell therein (for aye). They are the worst of creatures.." [Al-Bayyinah 98:6]

Many verses and Hadith express the same meaning. The one, who rejects the idea that the Jews and Christians who do not believe in Mohammed [peace be upon him] and deny him are disbelievers, is in fact denying what Allah has said. Denying what Allah has said is blasphemy. If anyone has any doubt concerning them being disbelievers, then he himself is also a disbeliever. This is a matter concerning which there is no room for doubt. And help is sought only with Allah.

Chapter I

THE MESSENGER AND THE MESSAGE

In the year A.D.610, in a cave near Mecca, while he was spending time in solitary meditation, Mohammed asserted that he was visited by the Angel Gabriel who in a vision delivered to him the first message of Islam.

1- MOHAMMED

Mohammed was born A.D. 570 into a highly regarded family from the respected tribe of Qoraysh. His father died before his birth and his mother died when he was only six years old. When he was eight, his grandfather Abdel Muttalib also died, leaving him in the care of his uncle, Abu Talib.

As a young man, Mohammed was exposed to the various sects of Christianity and Judaism. He observed how they were constantly arguing and debating one another. This may have influenced his disenchantment with the traditional polytheistic religion of the Arabs at that time. Mohammed later referred to Christians and Jews as "People of the Book." (In reference to the Bible)

At age 25, Mohammed worked as a trader in the service of the rich widow Khadija, who later married him. She was 15 years older than he. He then became a successful merchant.

At age 40, Mohammed spent much time in meditation, and proclaimed himself to be selected by God to preach the true religion. Mohammed very soon faced harassment and persecution from the tribal chiefs who saw the new religion as a danger to the city's principal source of revenue. They feared that it would eliminate the profitable pilgrimages to the pagan shrine of the Kaaba.

In the year A.D. 622, after an attempt by his opponents to murder him, Mohammed and his few followers fled to Yathrib (later named Medina) in a migration known as the Hijira.

In Medina, Mohammed's followers grew in strength and number. From there he began a series of raids on the city of Mecca. Ultimately he subjugated the city and brought all of Arabia under his control.

Mohammed died in the year A.D. 632.

2- ISLAM

The Arabic word "Islam" means "submission" [to God]. Islam claims that it was never a new religion, but rather a continuation and culmination of God's revelations to Noah, Abraham, Moses and Jesus.

To become a Muslim, one must accept and declare the creed of Islam, commonly known as the two professions of the faith. These are, *"there is no other God but Allah, and Mohammed is the messenger of Allah."* A Muslim then must believe in six articles of faith: God, the Angels, the Scriptures, the Prophets, the Day of Judgment, and Fatalism.

A Muslim must perform five religious duties known as "The Pillars of Islam," which are: The Professions, Prayer, Almsgiving, Fasting, and Pilgrimage to Mecca. Some have raised the Quranic sanction of Holy War (Jihad) for the spread of Islam to the rank of a sixth religious duty.

It is interesting to note that much of Islam's practices and rituals were borrowed from the pre-Islamic pagan Arabs. This is the period that Muslims refer to as "al-Jahilyya" (Ignorance Age). Some of these rituals are: exalting the Kaaba and the Black Stone, pilgrimage to Mecca, fasting Ramadan, dedicating Friday for assembling to worship, and adopting the name "Allah" for God.

3 - JIHAD (HOLY WAR)

"Jihad" is an Arabic word, which means, "struggle." Jihad in Islam can mean striving to be a better Muslim. The most common meaning, however, is the struggle for the cause of spreading Islam, using all means available to Muslims, including violence. This kind of Jihad is often referred to as *"Holy War."*

In resorting to violence, Muslims do not have a problem finding passages in the Quran and Hadith that do not only condone violence, but even demand it.

In the Quran, Allah orders Muslims to terrorize non-Muslims in His behalf:
> *"**Strike terror** (into the hearts of) the enemies of Allah and your enemies."* Surah 8:60

> *"**Fight (kill)** them (non Muslims) and Allah will **punish (torment)** them by your hands, cover them with shame."* Surah 9:14

> *"I will **instil terror** into the hearts of the unbelievers, **smite** ye above their necks and smite all their finger-tips off them. **It is not ye who slew them; it was Allah.**"* Surah 8:12,17

> *"O ye who believe! **Fight** the unbelievers...let them find firmness (harshness) in you and know that Allah is with those who fear Him."* Surah 9:123

In the Hadith (Mohammed's sayings), Mohammed also urges Muslims to practice Jihad:
Mohammed once was asked: what is the best deed for the Muslim next to believing in Allah and His Apostle? His answer was: *"To participate in **Jihad** in Allah's cause."* Al-Bukhari Vol. 1:25

Mohammed was also quoted as saying: *"I have been ordered to **fight** with the people till they say, none has the right to be worshipped but Allah."* Al-Bukhari Vol. 4:196

It is worth noting here that the words "fight" and "kill" have appeared in the Quran more frequently than the word "pray."

Islam teaches that people are divided into two different camps; _Dar al Islam_ (The abode of Islam), in reference to Muslims, and _Dar al Harb_ (The abode of war), in reference to non-Muslims. This means that Muslims who belong to _Dar al Islam_ are in a constant state of war with non-Muslims, who belong to _Dar al Harb_; until such time non-Muslims convert to Islam. In other words Muslims can never peacefully co-exist with non-Muslims.

Mohammed and Jihad: an example

The following is just one example of Jihad from the life of the prophet of Islam, Mohammed.

After _the war of the trench_, in which Mohammed was besieged by the Qurayshites, led by Abu Sofyan, it was alleged that the Jewish tribe Bani Qurayza agreed to provide help from within to Abu Sofyan's forces. Although the alleged help did not materialize and the siege eventually ended, nevertheless, Mohammed never forgave them for their willingness to help his enemies.

Muslims turned against Bani Qurayza and blocked their streets for twenty-five days. The Jewish tribe expressed readiness to accept surrender, to give up their belongings, and to depart from their homes.

Mohammed, however, would not consent to this, and instead appointed as an arbiter, Saad iben Moaz, a man who was known to be on bad terms with Bani Qurayza. Saad ruled that all Bani Quaryza's men should be beheaded, that the women and children should be sold as slaves, and that all their property should be divided among the Muslims.

Trenches were dug in the bazaar of Medina for disposal of the approximately nine hundred Jewish bodies whom Mohammed and his followers had spent the previous night slaughtering. (See Ibn Hisham: The Prophet's Biography; Vol. 2, pages 240 & 241).

Chapter II

THE ISSUES
According to the "Quran"

Islam is more than a religion; it is a comprehensive way of life. The Quran, Mohammed, his immediate followers, and generations of theologians prescribed numerous regulations governing every aspect of Muslim social, political, economic, and religious life.

In this chapter we will examine only a few of these Islamic regulations, based on the most reliable source of all Islamic teachings, the Quran. The reader must determine whether or not it is acceptable to live under such teachings.

1-WOMEN'S RIGHTS

Are women equal to men according to Islam?
• Islam teaches that women are inferior to men.

> *"...And women shall have rights similar to the rights against them, according to what is equitable; but **men** have a degree over them..."*   Surah 2:228

In what areas are women unequal to men in Islam?
• Islam teaches that women are less than equal to men in at least two major areas:

First, in inheritance: A woman's share is half that of a man.

> *"To the **male** a portion equal to that of **two** females..."*
>   Surah 4:11

Second, in court witness: The witness of two women equals the witness of one man.
> *"And get two witnesses out of your own men, and if there are*

*not two men, then a man and **two women** such as ye choose, for witness..."*   Surah 2:282

What is the status of a wife in relation to her husband?
• Islam considers the wife a possession.

> *"...Fair in the eyes of men is the love of **things** they covet: **Women** and sons; heaped-up hoards of gold and silver; horses..."*   Surah 3:14

• Islam teaches that women are unclean. If a Muslim man touches a woman (even his wife) before praying, he is considered unclean for prayer.

> *"O ye who believe! Approach not prayers with a mind befogged until ye can understand all that ye say, nor in a state of ceremonial impurity (except when traveling on the road), until after washing your whole body if ye are ill or on a journey or one of you cometh from offices of nature, or ye have been in **contact with women**, and ye find no water, then take for yourselves clean sand or earth, and rub therewith your faces and hands: for Allah doth blot out sins and forgive again and again."*   Surah 4:43 (See also Surah 5:6)

What is the extent of a husband's authority over his wife in Islam?
• Islam teaches that a wife is subject to punishment by her husband. As a punishment, beating a wife or abstaining from sexual relations with her is allowed.

> *"...As to those women on whose part ye fear disloyalty and ill-conduct, **Admonish** them, **refuse to share their beds, beat them**,...."*   Surah 4:34

> *"For those who take an oath for **abstention** from their wives, a waiting for four months is ordained; if they return, God is oft-forgiving, most merciful."*   Surah 2:226

What rules apply only to women regarding appearance in public?

• Islam instructs women to veil themselves always when they are outside their homes. And, even inside their homes, in certain situations.

*"And say to the believing women that they should lower their gaze and guard their modesty; that they should not display their beauty and ornaments except what appear thereof; that they should draw their **veils over their bosoms** and not display their beauty..."* Surah 24:31

*"O prophet! Tell thy wives and daughters, and the believing women, that they should **cast their outer garments over their persons** (when abroad)..."* Surah 33:59

2 - SEX AND MARRIAGE

How many wives can a Muslim man marry?

• Islam allows polygamy: A man may marry up to four wives at one time.

*"...Marry women of your choice, **two**, or **three**, or **four**..."*

Surah 4:3

Note: Extra privileges were given to Mohammed, "The Prophet of Islam." He was allowed unlimited wives. Mohammed had at least 13 wives in addition to several concubines which we know of for a fact.

Ayesha was only nine years old at the time he married her, Mohammed was fifty-three years old. Another wife, Zaynab Bint Jahsh, was his daughter-in-law. When Zaid, Mohammed's adopted son, saw that Mohammed desired his wife, he divorced her so that Mohammed could marry her.

What is the sexual role of the wife in marriage according to Islam?
• Islam considers the wife a sex object.

> *"Your wives are as a **tilth** (a field to be ploughed) unto you, so approach your tilth when or **how ye will**."* Surah 2:223

Is divorce allowed in Islam?
• A man can divorce his wife by oral pronouncement. The wife has no such right in the Quran.

> *"It may be, if he **divorced** you that Allah will give him in exchange consorts better than you..."* Surah 66:5

May a man reunite with his wife after divorcing her?
• When a husband has pronounced divorce three times on his wife, he may not lawfully remarry her until she has married (and had sexual intercourse) and been divorced by another man called "Al Mohalil" (the legalizer).

> *"A divorce is only **permissible** twice; after that, the parties should either hold together on equitable terms, or separate with kindness,..."* Surah 2:229

> "...So if a husband divorces his wife he cannot after that, remarry her until after she has married **another husband**, and he has divorced her, in that case there is no blame on either of them if they reunite..." Surah 2:230

3 - HUMAN RIGHTS

Does Islam permit freedom of choice regarding religion?
• Islam compels its adherents to force others to accept Islam. Muslims must fight until all their opponents submit to Islam, unless, of course, those opponents prefer death. Christians and Jews may be spared if they pay the "Jizya" (penalty tax) with willing submission, and humiliation.

*"**Fight** those who believe not in Allah nor the last day... Nor acknowledge the religion of truth, (even if they are) of the people of the Book, until they pay the Jizya (taxes) with willing submission, and feel themselves subdued."*

Surah 9:29

*"But when the forbidden months are past, then **fight** and **slay** the pagans wherever ye find them and seize them, **beleaguer them, and lie in wait (ambush) for them** in every stratagem (of war); but if they repent and establish regular prayers and practice regular charity then open the way for them."*

Surah 9:5 (see also Surah 2:193)

*"Therefore; when ye meet the unbelievers (in fight) **smite** at their necks; at length, when ye have thoroughly **subdued** them, bind a bond firmly in (on them): thereafter (is the time for) either generosity or ransom, until the war lays down its burdens."*

Surah 47:4

Does Islam teach the equality of all people?

• Islam teaches that Muslims are superior to others.

*"Ye (Muslims) are the **best of peoples**, evolved for mankind..."*

Surah 3:110

• Allah is said to have transformed some non-Muslims into apes and swine.

*"(O people of the Book) Say: shall I point out to you something much worse than this, (as judged) by the treatment it received from Allah? Those who incurred the curse of Allah and His wrath, those of whom some **He transformed into apes and swine**..."*

Surah 5:60

Can Islam co-exist with and tolerate other religions?

• Islam condemns non-Muslims, other than Christians and Jews, as infidels.

> *"The life of this world is alluring to those who **reject faith** (infidels), and they scoff at those who believe. But the righteous will be above them on the day of resurrection..."*
>
> Surah 2:212

• Neither do Christians and Jews escape Islam's condemnation.

> *"The Jews call Uzair a son of Allah, and the Christians call Christ the son of Allah. That is a saying from their mouths; (in this) they but imitate what the **unbelievers** (infidels) of old used to say. **Allah's curse be on them**: how they are deluded away from the truth!"*
>
> Surah 9:30

• Islam instructs Muslims to not befriend Jews or Christians.

> *"O ye who believe! **Take not the Jews and the Christians for your friends** and protectors. They are but friends and protectors to each other. And he amongst you that turns to them (for friendship) is of them. Verily, Allah guideth not a people unjust."*
>
> Surah 5:51

What happens to a person who converts to Islam and then later changes his mind?

• Islam teaches that any person who accepts Islam and then later turns away from it will be subject to death.

> *"But if they violate their oaths after their covenant, and taunt you for your faith, fight ye the chiefs of unfaith: for their oaths are nothing to them."*
>
> Surah 9:12 (See also Surah 4:89)

4 -DEMOCRACY

Does Islam teach the "Separation of Church and State?"
• Islam teaches that the Quran is the Constitution, God is the author of law, and the State is the agent, which implements the law.

*"And **fight** them on, until there is no more tumult or oppression, and there prevail justice and faith **in Allah** (and the religion becomes that of Allah)."*　　　　　Surah 2:193

*"We have sent down to thee **the Book in truth**, that thou mightest judge between men, **as guided by Allah**: so be not as an advocate by those who betray their trust."*　　　Surah 4:105

*"So judge between them by **what Allah hath revealed** and follow not their vain desires, diverging from the truth that has come to thee. To each among you have we prescribed a law and open way."*　　　　　　　　　　　　Surah 5:48

*"The command (the rule) **is for none but Allah**; He hath commanded that ye worship none but Him: That is the right religion, but most men understand not."*　　　Surah 12:40

How Does the Quran consider those who do not abide by its laws?
• The Quran considers them wrong-doers, rebels, and unbelievers.

*"And if any fail to judge by what Allah hath revealed, they are **wrong-doers**."*　　　　　　　　　　　　Surah 5:45

*"If any do fail to judge by what Allah hath revealed, they are those who **rebel**."*　　　　　　　　　　　Surah 5:47

*"If any do fail to judge by what Allah hath revealed, they are **unbelievers**."*　　　　　　　　　　　　Surah 5:44

What are some of Islamic rules and punishments that must be implemented within an Islamic State?

• Islam imposes a harsh code of punishment on those who violate its laws. Here are some examples:

Resisting Islam: punished by death, crucifixion or the cutting off of the hands and feet.

> *"The punishment of those who wage war against Allah and His Messenger, and strive with might and main for mischief through the land is: **execution, or crucifixion, or the cutting off of the hands and feet** from opposite sides or exile from the land..."* Surah 5:33

Adultery and Fornication: Sex outside marriage is punished by public flogging for the unmarried person. For the married, the punishment is stoning.

> *"The woman and the man guilty of adultery or fornication, **flog** each of them with a hundred stripes; let not compassion move you in their case, in a matter prescribed by Allah, if ye believe in Allah and the Last Day; and let a party of the believers witness their punishment."* Surah 24:2

Stealing: punished by amputation of the hands.

> *"As to the thief, male or female, **cut off** his or her hands: A punishment, by way of example, from Allah for their crime: and Allah is exalted in power."* Surah 5:38

Drinking: punished by 40 to 80 lashes according to the Hadith (Mohammed's sayings). See Sahih al-Bukhari Vol. 8:770

> *"O ye who believe! Intoxicants and gambling, stones and arrows, are an abomination, of Satan's handiwork: Eschew such that you may prosper."* Surah 5:90

Would these laws be imposed on non-Muslim minorities in an Islamic State?

• Non-Muslims must follow the same rules, and are subject to the same punishment.

> *"If anyone desires a religion other than Islam, never will it be accepted of him; and in the hereafter he will be in the ranks of those who have lost."*   Surah 3:85

Would an opposition party be allowed in an Islamic State?

• No, because the ruler rules by a mandate from Allah, and Allah must not be opposed.

> *"Whatever it be wherein ye differ, **the decision** (the rule) **thereof is with Allah**: such is Allah my Lord: In Him I trust, and to Him I turn."*   Surah 42:10

> *"O ye who believe obey Allah and obey the Messenger and those charged with authority among you. **If you differ in anything among yourselves, refer it to Allah** and His Messenger."*
> Surah 4:59

Has the experiment of an Islamic State been applied in modern history? If so, how successful has it been?

• There are many countries today that rule, to different degrees, by Islamic laws. Some of the countries that rigidly apply Islam are: Afghanistan, Saudi Arabia, Iran, Sudan and Pakistan. The condition of these countries speaks for itself; **human rights violations, violence and terrorism, oppression and persecution. Most Islamic countries are economically bankrupt.**

5 - ETERNAL SECURITY

How sure can a Muslim be about his eternity?

• Islam teaches that "fate" decides everyone's eternal destination.

> *"Every man's **fate** We have fastened on his own neck: on the day of Judgment We shall bring out for him a scroll which he will see spread open."*   Surah 17:13

- The Quran teaches that every Muslim will pass through hell.

*"Not one of you but will **pass over it** (originally: **through** it [hell]). This is a decree which must be accomplished."*

Surah 19:71

- The only assurance for a Muslim that he will go to Paradise is through fighting for the cause of spreading Islam and being martyred in the process.

"And if ye are slain, or die in the way of Allah, forgiveness and mercy from Allah are far better than all they could amass."

Surah 3:157

Does the God of Islam lead each Muslim to eternal salvation?

- According to the Quran, God leads and misleads as He pleases.

"Allah leaves straying those whom He pleases and guides whom He pleases."   Surah 14:4

*"Those whom Allah willeth to guide, **He openeth** their breast to Islam; Those whom He willeth to leave straying, **He maketh their breast close** and constricted as if they had to climb up to the skies."*

Surah 6:125

- God's will is that some be not guided aright, but He will inflict punishment on them for not being guided aright.

"If We had so willed, We could certainly have brought every soul its true guidance: But the word from Me will come true "I will fill hell with jinns (demons) and men all together."

Surah 32:13

- God makes it impossible for those who reject Islam to believe later.

"As to those who reject faith, it is the same to them whether

28

thou warn them or do not warn them; they will not believe.
Allah hath set a seal on their hearts *and on their hearing, and on their eyes is a veil; great is the penalty they (incur)."*

Surah 2:6, 7

• God orders people to transgress so that He will have an excuse to destroy them.

"When We decide to destroy a population, **We (first) send a definite order** *to those among them who are given the good things of this life and yet* **transgress,** *(in the original: and they transgressed) so that the word is proved true against them: then (it is)* **We destroy** *them utterly."* Surah 17:16

• It is up to Allah, the all powerful, to punish or forgive whomever He pleaseth, whenever He pleaseth.

"He (Allah) forgiveth whom He pleaseth, and punisheth whom He pleaseth, for Allah hath power over all things."

Surah 2:284

What is Islam's concept of heaven?
• Heaven in Islam is the place where a Muslim man will be reclining, eating meat and delicious fruits, drinking exquisite wines, and engaging in sex with beautiful women, and eternally-young beautiful boys or young men *"Wildan or Gholman."* There is no mention of women's rewards.

It is interesting to note that many of the things that are forbidden to Muslims here on earth are allowed to them in abundance in Paradise. Some of these things are drinking wine, practicing homosexuality and engaging in sex every day with dozens of virgins (whom Allah will automatically restore their virginity).

"As to the righteous, they will be in gardens, and in happiness... *(to them will be said:)* "Eat and drink ye, with profit and health, because of your (good) deeds." They will recline (with ease) on thrones (of dignity) arranged in ranks; and We shall join them*

(in the original: marry them) to companions with beautiful, big and lustrous eyes... And We shall bestow on them, of fruit and meat, anything they desire. They shall there exchange, one with another, a cup free of frivolity, free of all taint of ill. Round about them will serve to them young male servants (handsome) as pearls well-guarded."   Surah 52:17, 19, 20, 22-24

"(Here is) a Parable of the Garden which the righteous are promised: in it are rivers of water incorruptible; rivers of milk of which the taste never changes; rivers of wine, a joy to those who drink; and rivers of honey pure and clear. In it there are for them all kinds of fruits; and Grace from their Lord. (Can those in such Bliss) be compared to such as shall dwell for ever in the Fire, and be given, to drink, boiling water, so that it cuts up their bowels (to pieces)"   Surah 47:15

"Verily for the Righteous there will be a fulfillment of (the heart's) desires,   Gardens enclosed, and grapevines; And voluptuous women of equal age; And a cup full (to the brim)."   Surah 78: 31-34

"We have created (their Companions) of special creation. And made them virgin - pure (and undefiled), Beloved (by nature), equal in age For the Companions of the Right Hand"   Surah 56:35-38

"Verily the Companions of the Garden shall that Day have joy in all that they do; They and their associates will be in groves of (cool) shade, reclining on Thrones (of dignity)."   Surah 36:55, 56

(See also Surah 4:57; Surah 76:12-22; and Surah 55:54-56)

Chapter III

THE ISSUES
According to the "Hadith"

The "Hadith" is a record of Mohammed's words and deeds according to his wives, relatives, and companions. The "Hadith" is viewed by Muslims as inspired. Next to the Quran, it is the most important part of Islamic law; its teachings are just as binding.

All of our quotes here are from "Sahih Al-Bukhari" which comes in nine volumes and contains thousands of Hadiths, which are recognized by Muslims to be authentic. Limited space will allow us to mention just a few examples.

Our purpose is to give the reader a taste of the teachings of Mohammed. Some of these teachings may shock you; some may amuse you. Others may simply leave you mystified!

1 - WOMEN'S RIGHTS

• **Women are to be veiled.**
   "He (Umar) desired eagerly that the verses of Al Hijab (observing of veils by Muslim women) be revealed. So Allah revealed the verses of Al-Hijab."   Vol. 1:148

• **Women are deficient in mind and religion.**
   Mohammed asked some women, *"Isn't the witness of a woman equal to half of that of a man?"* The women said, *"yes"*. He said, *"This is because of the deficiency of the woman's mind."*
   Vol. 3:826

   Mohammed to women: *"I have not seen any one more deficient in intelligence and religion than you."*   Vol. 2:541

- **The majority of people in hell are women.**
  Mohammed said, *"I was shown the Hell-fire and that the majority of its dwellers are women."*

  Vol. 1:28, 301; Vol. 2:161; Vol. 7:124

- **Women are bad omens.**
  Mohammed said, *"Bad omen is in the woman, the house and the horse."* Vol. 7:30

- **Women are harmful to men.**
  Mohammed said, *"After me I have not left any affliction more harmful to men than women."* Vol. 7:33

- **Women may not wear wigs.**
  Mohammed said, *"Don't wear false hair for Allah sends His curse upon such ladies who lengthen their hair artificially."*

  Vol. 7:133

2 - SEX AND MARRIAGE

- **Mohammed's sexual strength was equal to 30 men.**
  Anas said, *"The prophet used to visit all his wives in an hour round, during the day and night and they were eleven in number."* I asked Anas, *"Had the prophet the strength for it?"* Anas replied, *"We used to say that the prophet was given the strength of thirty (men)."* Vol. 1:268

- **Allah hurried to please Mohammed's sexual desires.**
  When the Quranic verse that allowed Mohammed to postpone the turn of any of his wives was revealed, and when Mohammed said that Allah allowed him to marry his adopted son's wife, Aisha (one of his wives) said, *"O Allah's Apostle I do not see but that your Lord hurries in pleasing you."*

  Vol. 7:48

- **When a woman is divorced irrevocably, she can not return to her husband until she marries another man**

(including having sexual intercourse with him).

"Narrated Aisha: The wife of Rifaa Al-Qurazi came to Allah's Apostle and said, "O Allah's Apostle, Rifaa divorced me irrevocably. After him I married Abdur-Rahman bin Az-Zubair Al-Qurazi who proved to be impotent." Allah's Apostle said to her, "Perhaps you want to return to Rifaa? Nay (you cannot return to Rifaa) until you and Abdur-Rahman (the impotent man) engage in sexual intercourse!"   Vol. 7:186

3 - HUMAN RIGHTS

* **Islam is to be imposed by force.**
  Mohammed said, *"I have been ordered to fight with the people till they say,* **"None has the right to be worshipped but Allah,** *and whoever says, 'None has the right to be worshipped but Allah, his life and property will be saved by me."* (Otherwise it will not).   Vol. 4:196

* **Apostacy is punishable by death.**
  Mohammed said, *"Whoever changes his (Islamic) religion, kill him."*   Vol. 9:57

* **A Muslim should not be killed if he kills a non-Muslim.**
  Mohammed said, *"No Muslim should be killed for killing a kafir"* (infidel).   Vol. 9:50

* **Ethnic cleansing is permitted.**
  Mohammed said to the Jews, *"You should know that the earth belongs to Allah and His Apostle (Mohammed) and I want to expel you from this land (the Arabian Peninsula), so, if anyone owns property, he is permitted to sell it."*   Vol. 4:392

  Mohammed's last words at his deathbed were: *"Turn the pagans (non-Muslims) out of the Arabian Peninsula."*
      Vol. 5:716

4 - ETERNAL SECURITY

- **There is no assurance of salvation.**
  Mohammed said, *"By Allah, though I am the apostle of Allah, yet **I do not know what Allah will do to me**."*   Vol. 5:266

- **God punishes a deceased person if his relatives weep.**
  Mohammed said, *"The deceased is punished because of the weeping of his relatives."*   Vol. 2:375

- **When you speak badly about a deceased person, the deceased person will go to hell.**
  Mohammed said, *"You praised this, so paradise has been affirmed to him, and you spoke badly of this, so Hell has been affirmed to him, You people are Allah's witnesses on Earth."*
  Vol. 2:448

- **Urine on your clothes will bring punishment in the after-life.**
  Mohammed said, *"The deceased person is being tortured in the grave not for a great thing to avoid, it is for being soiled with his urine."*   Vol. 2:460

- **The sword is the key to heaven.**
  Mohammed said, *"Know that Paradise is under the shades of swords."*   Vol. 4:73

- **Holy War (Jihad) is the guarantee of heaven.**
  Mohammed said, *"The person who participates in Holy Battles in Allah's cause and nothing compels him to do so except belief in Allah and His Apostle, **will be recompensed by Allah either with a reward, or booty (if he survives) or will be admitted to Paradise (if he is killed)**."*   Vol. 1:35

5 - MEDICINE

- **Drinking camel's urine will make you healthy.**
  "The prophet ordered them to follow his camels, and drink their milk and urine, so they followed the camels and drank their milk and urine till their bodies became healthy."
  Vol. 7:590

- **Fever is from the heat of hell.**
  Mohammed said, *"Fever is from the heat of hell, so put it out (cool it) with water."*
  Vol. 7:619

- **A fly in your drink is a cure.**
  Mohammed said, *"If a housefly falls in the drink of anyone of you, he should dip it (in the drink), for one of its wings has a disease and the other has the cure for the disease."* Vol. 4:537

- **How the baby's looks are determined.**
  Mohammed said, *"As for the child, if the man's discharge precedes the woman's discharge, the child attracts the similarity of the man, and if the woman's discharge precedes the man's, then the child attracts the similarity of the woman."*
  Vol. 5:275

6 - MISCELLANEOUS

- **If you eat garlic don't come to the place of worship.**
  Mohammed said, *"Whoever ate from this plant (i.e. garlic) should not enter our mosque."*
  Vol. 1:812

- **The evil eye has a definite effect.**
  Mohammed said, *"The effect of an evil eye is a fact."*
  Vol. 7:636

- **Which shoe you should put on first.**
  Mohammed said, *"If you want to put on your shoes, put on the*

right shoe first, and if you want to take them off, take the left one first." Vol. 7:747

- ## Breathing in your drink is bad.
  Mohammed said, *"Don't breathe into your drinking utensil."* Vol. 1:156

- ## God frightens his devotees with eclipse.
  Mohammed said, *"The sun and the moon are two signs amongst the signs of Allah and they do not eclipse because of the death of someone but Allah frightens His devotees with them."* Vol. 2:158

- ## Satan urinates in people's ears, when they don't wake up for prayer.
  "Narrated Abdullah: the prophet was told that a person had kept on sleeping till morning and had not got up for the prayer. The prophet said, "Satan urinated in his ears." Vol. 2:245

- ## Yawning is from Satan.
  The prophet said, *"Yawning is from Satan and if anyone of you yawns, he should check his yawning as much as possible, for if anyone of you (during the act of yawning) should say: 'Ha', Satan will laugh at him."* Vol. 4:509

- ## Stars are missiles which God uses to hit the devils.
  "The creation of these stars is for three purposes, i.e. as decoration of the sky, as missiles to hit the devils, and as signs to guide travelers." Vol. 4:420

Chapter IV
THE DIFFERENCE

1 -CHRISTIANITY VS. ISLAM

How do the teachings of Christianity, on the issues we discussed in the last two chapters, compare with the teachings of Islam?

Here are some sample statements of what Christianity teaches:

Women's Rights
- Women are equal to men.   Galatians 3:28
- Husbands are called to love their wives.   Ephesians 5:25-29
- Women have the same rights as men.   1 Corinthians 11:11

Sex and Marriage
- The Bible makes it clear that monogamy is God's plan for marriage.   Matthew 19:4-6

- Abstaining from sexual relations is permitted by the husband and wife only for a short time, mutually agreed upon, and for the specific purpose of prayer.   1 Corinthians 7:5

- Divorce is not allowed except in the case of adultery.
                            Matthew 5:32; Matthew 19:3-5 & 9

- Anyone who divorces his wife, except for marital unfaithfulness, and marries another woman commits adultery.   Matthew 19:9

Human Rights
- Every person has the freedom to accept the gift of salvation in Jesus Christ, or reject it.   John 1:12; Luke 10:8-10

- The Bible does not favor any race over another.
                            Galatians 3:28; Colossians 3:11

• The God of the Bible extends His love to all people; Jesus Christ died on the cross to pay for the sin of the whole world.   John 3:16

• Christ commands His followers to love everyone, even their enemies.   Matthew 5:43-48

• Christians are instructed not to condemn others. Romans 14:4

Democracy
• Christianity distinguishes between Church and State, God and Caesar (Government).   Luke 20:25

• Christianity is a spiritual religion. It does not impose rules and regulations on society. Jesus was concerned about changing people's hearts. When the individual is changed, society will change also.   John 6:63; 10:10

• Christianity does not aspire to rule, but teaches that we are to be subject to rulers and authorities regardless of their religion.
Titus 3:1; 1 Timothy 2:1-4

• Christians are instructed not to judge or punish those who reject their views.   1 Peter 3:9; Luke 6:37

Eternal Security
• Each person is certain of his eternal destination through believing in Jesus Christ.   2 Timothy 1:12

• God's will for man is always for his good.   Romans 8:28

• God calls on everyone to believe. John 3:16; Romans 10: 9-13

• No condemnation can fall upon those who come in faith to Christ Jesus.   Romans 8:1

• Heaven's pleasures are pleasures of the spirit, pleasures of purity.   Matthew 22:30; Revelation 22:1-5

2 - THE BIBLE VS. THE QURAN

The Quran is the Muslims' Holy Book, as the Bible is to the Christians. Muslims regard the Quran as the infallible utterance of the Almighty. The word "Quran" means recitation. The name was applied by Mohammed for each individual portion of the Book, but was later used for the whole Book.

Mohammed proclaimed the Quran as the miracle that proved his prophethood. **There has been, however, much debate among intellectual Muslims on the issue of the miracle of the Quran. Some Arabic scholars like Zamakhshari noted more than one hundred grammatical errors in the Quran.**

The Quran is written in Arabic poetic prose. It is divided into 114 Surahs or chapters, and contains the religious, social, civil, commercial, military, and legal code of Islam. It also contains stories which occur in the Jewish and Christian Scriptures and Apocrypha.

The Quran, however, contradicts the Bible in many of the details of these stories, including some of the names of the people involved. When faced by these contradictions, Muslims justify them by claiming that the Bible must have been altered. Yet in no place in the Quran do we find the Omniscient (knowing everything) Allah pointing out these altered passages of the Bible or revealing the correct ones. Such a claim can also be disputed by historical evidence, as well as by the Quran itself, which approved of the Bible, and said so repeatedly:
> *"O ye People of the Book! Believe in what We have (now) revealed, confirming what was (already) with you..."*
> Surah 4:47 (see also Surah 2:40, 41, 91; 20:133; 26:192-198; 29:47 and 46:10-12).

There is enough evidence to support the claim that the Quran may have been tampered with. Nobody knows where the original Quran is. The Quran that we have in our hands now is called Uthman's

Quran, which was collected by Uthman, long after Mohammed's death. Parts of the original Quran must have been lost, after many of the reciters of the Quran died or were killed in battle. Uthman, the third Caliph (successor of Mohammed), gathered what was left of the Quran, arranged it by the length of Surahs rather than chronologically, then burned all other existing copies. **One would have to wonder: why Uthman burned all existing copies of the Quran if he didn't have something to hide?!**

The Bible, on the other hand, has stood the test of time. To suggest that the Bible has been altered is against both reason and historical findings.

Neither Christians nor Jews can reasonably be accused of altering their Scriptures. One reason is that they didn't have anything to gain from doing so, and if they did, they wouldn't willingly spill their blood defending it. In the book of Revelation God puts a severe punishment on those who add to or take away any part of God's word.

> *"For I testify unto every man that heareth the words of the prophecy of this book, if any man shall add unto these things, God shall add unto him the plagues that are written in this book: And if any man shall take away from the words of the book of this prophecy, God shall take away his part of the book of life, and out of the holy city, and from the things which are written in this book."*   Revelation 22:18 & 19

The Jews were also commanded not to commit such a terrible act.

> *"You shall not add unto the word which I command you, neither shall you diminish aught from it, that ye may keep the commandments of the Lord, your God, which I command you."*   Deuteronomy 4:2

Furthermore, historical and scientific evidence shows that Christians and Jews did not alter their Scriptures. Many manuscripts of early copies of the Bible were discovered through the years, and were found to match the text we have now. Here are some of these famous manuscripts:

The Sinaitic - Written in the middle of the fourth century, about 270 years before Islam. It contains the whole New Testament and a large part of the Old Testament, and is now kept in the British Museum.

The Alexandrian - Written in the early fifth century, more than 200 years before Islam. It contains the whole Bible, except a few pages that have been lost, and is kept in the British Museum.

The Vatican - It was written in the early fourth century, about 300 years before Islam. It contains the whole Bible, and is now kept in the Vatican Library at Rome.

These and other manuscripts such as *Codex Ephraemi* and the *Dead Sea Scrolls* and the thousands of other copies and parts of copies of the early Bibles prove beyond doubt that the Bible could not possibly have been altered or corrupted.

CAN GOD CONTRADICT HIMSELF?

Many stories of the Bible that have been recorded in the Quran are contradictory to the Bible. Here are a few examples:

The story of Cain and Abel
After Cain killed his brother Abel, The Quran says, *"Allah sent a raven who scratched the ground to show him how to hide the shame of his brother."* Surah 5:31. This is not mentioned in the Bible.

The story of Noah and the flood
1. The Quran in Surah 11:42 & 43 says that one of the sons of Noah refused to go into the Ark and was drowned in the flood, while the Bible says that all three sons of Noah went into the Ark with him and were saved from the flood (Genesis 7:7).

2. In Surah 11:44 the Quran says that the Ark came to rest on

top of mount Judi, while the Bible says it was Mount Ararat (Genesis 8:4).

The Story of Abraham
1.   Abraham's father, according to the Quran, is Azar (Surah 6:74) while the Bible says that his name was Terah (Genesis 11:26).

2.   The Quran says Abraham had two sons, the Bible says they were eight.

3.   The Quran says some of Abraham's descendants lived in the valley of Mecca (Surah 14:37), while the Bible says they lived in Hebron (Genesis 13:18).

4.   The Quran says that Abraham had two wives, the Bible says he had three.

5.   The Quran says that he built the Kaaba (Surah 2:125-127), the Bible has no record of that.

The story of Moses
1.   The Quran states that the one who adopted Moses was Pharaoh's wife (Surah 28:9), while the Bible says it was Pharaoh's daughter (Exodus 2:5).

2.   The Quran states that Haman lived in Egypt during Moses' time (Surah 28:6), while the Bible says that he lived in Persia during King Ahasuerus time (Esther 3:1).

The story of Mary (the mother of Jesus)
1.   The Quran states that Mary's brother was Aaron (Surah 19: 28), while the Bible says that Aaron lived 1300 years before Mary. (Numbers 26:59)

2.   The Quran states that Mary gave birth to Jesus under a palm tree (Surah 19:23), while the Bible says it was in a stable. (Luke 2:7)

3. The Quran states that Jesus spoke and performed miracles at the time he was just a baby (Surah 19:24-26), the Bible has no record of that.

4. The Quran states that Zacharias could not speak for three nights (Surah 19:10), while the Bible says that he could not speak until the child was born (or for about 9 months). (Luke 1:20)

CAN GOD MAKE THESE ERRORS?

Muslims believe that the Quran is a direct utterance of Allah (God). Because God is infallible, one would expect the Quran to be infallible also. However, by examining the Quran, we are faced by many statements that go against the undisputed facts of science. It would be unacceptable if such errors were attributed to a learned human being, worse yet to attribute them to the Omniscient God. The list of the errors in the Quran is very long, and are discussed in full detail in other books. Here, we have a limited space to list only a few samples. Our goal is to question whether God can make such errors, whether God was in fact the author of the Quran.

Geographical Errors

The Earth is stationary
"He created the heavens without any pillars that ye can see; He set on the earth mountains standing firm, lest it should shake with you; and He scattered through it beasts of all kinds. We send down rain from the sky, and produce on the earth every kind of noble creature, in pairs." Surah 31:10

The Sun sets in a spring
"Until, when he reached the setting of the sun, he found it set in a spring of murky water: Near it he found a People: We said: "O Zul-qarnain! (thou hast authority,) either to punish them, or to treat them with kindness." Surah 18:86

Historical Errors

Pharaoh built the tower of Babel in Egypt

"Pharaoh said: "O Chiefs! no god do I know for you but myself: therefore, O Haman! light me a (kiln to bake bricks) out of clay, and build me a lofty palace, that I may mount up to the god of Moses: but as far as I am concerned, I think (Moses) is a liar!"

Surah 28:38

Alexander the Great was a prophet

"They ask thee concerning Zul-qarnain (Alexander the Great) Say, "I will rehearse to you something of his story." Verily We established his power on earth, and We gave him the ways and the means to all ends. One (such) way he followed, Until, when he reached the setting of the sun, he found it set in a spring of murky water: Near it he found a People: We said: "O Zul-qarnain! (thou hast authority,) either to punish them, or to treat them with kindness."
Surah 18:83-88

Ethical Errors

Legalizing perjury

"Allah will not call you to account for thoughtlessness in your oaths, but for the intention in your hearts; and He is Oft-forgiving, Most Forbearing."

Surah 2:225

Legalizing murder

"O Prophet! Rouse the Believers to the fight. If there are twenty amongst you, patient and persevering, they will vanquish two hundred: if a hundred, they will vanquish a thousand of the Unbelievers: for these are a people without understanding."

Surah 8:65

Legalizing deceit

"Allah will not call you to account for what is futile in your oaths, but He will call you to account for your deliberate oaths: for expiation, feed ten indigent persons, on a scale of the average for the food of your families; or clothe them; or give a slave his

freedom. If that is beyond your means, fast for three days. That is the expiation for the oaths ye have sworn. But keep to your oaths. Thus doth God make clear to you His signs, that ye may be grateful." Surah 5:89

Scientific Errors

A corpse leaning on a staff for a year
"Then, when We decreed (Solomon's) death, nothing showed them his death except a little worm of the earth, which kept (slowly) gnawing away at his staff: so when he fell down, the Jinns saw plainly that if they had known the unseen, they would not have tarried in the humiliating Penalty (of their Task)." Surah 34:14

A nap lasting three hundred and nine years
"So they stayed in their Cave three hundred years, and (some) add nine (more)" Surah 18:9-26

Legal Errors

Scourging the witness
"And those who launch a charge against chaste women, and produce not four witnesses (to support their allegations),- flog them with eighty stripes; and reject their evidence ever after: for such men are wicked transgressors." Surah 24:4

God ordains taking spoils
"And know that out of all the booty that ye may acquire (in war), a fifth share is assigned to God,- and to the Messenger, and to near relatives, orphans, the needy, and the wayfarer,- if ye do believe in Allah and in the revelation We sent down to Our servant on the Day of Testing,- the Day of the meeting of the two forces. For Allah hath power over all things." Surah 8:41

****

Since the Bible came first, and since there is every reason to believe that the Bible was kept uncorrupted, Muslim theologians

45

have much explaining to do with regard to these contradictions and errors in their Book.

3 - GOD vs. ALLAH

Both Christians and Muslims share belief in a sovereign Deity who is one, heavenly, spiritual, the creator of heaven and earth and the judge of all mankind. Muslims call Him *"Allah"*. One may thus presume that God of Christianity and Allah of Islam are the same. A careful examination of the matter, however, will prove that it is not exactly so.

Muslim activists in the West have been using the tactic of claiming that they worship the same god as the Christians in order to gain legitimacy and acceptance.

There is nothing new under the sun! This reminds us of what happened 14 centuries ago. When Mohammed started preaching his new religion in Mecca he was conciliatory and appeasing to Christians. He told them: *"We believe in the revelation which has come down to us and which came down to you, **our Allah and your Allah is one**."* Surah 29:46. Compare this with what happened later, in Medina, after Mohammed gained strength. Allah then tells him to:

*"**Fight those who believe not in Allah nor the last day...Nor acknowledge the religion of truth (Islam), (even if they are) of the people of the Book, until they pay the Jizya (tribute tax) with willing submission, and feel themselves subdued**."* Surah 9:29

THE GOD OF CHRISTIANITY
Christianity believes in a one triune God, while Islam rejects this concept as blasphemous.

> *"They do **blaspheme** who say Allah is one of three in a **Trinity**, for there is no god except **One Allah**."* Surah 5:73

The reason behind Islam's rejection of the concept of the triune God is a misunderstanding of the real meaning behind it. It seems that Islam's understanding of the Trinity was derived from a heresy which existed in Arabia at the time of Mohammed. This heresy taught a trinity consisting of God the Father, God the Mother (the Virgin Mary), and God the Son (Jesus). The Quran says:

*"And behold! Allah will say: O Jesus the son of Mary didst thou say unto men, **worship me and my mother as gods** in derogation of Allah? He (Jesus) will say: Glory to thee, never could I say what I had no right (to say)."*

Surah 5:116

Christians, in fact, believe in one God who has made Himself manifest in three Persons: Father, Son, and Holy Spirit. Jesus declared this doctrine when He instructed His disciples, saying:

*"Go ye therefore, and teach all nations, baptizing them in the name of the **Father, and of the Son, and of the Holy Ghost**."*

Matthew 28:19 & 20

The Father

Islam doesn't know the loving Fatherhood of God. That intimate relationship with God is foreign to Islam and condemned by the Quran.

*"(Both) the Jews and the Christians say, 'We are **sons of Allah** and His beloved.' Say: why then doth He punish you for your sins? Nay, you are but men of the men He has created."*

Surah 5:18

On the other hand, the concept of God being our heavenly Father is at the core of the Christian faith. Jesus taught His disciples to pray, saying:

*"**Our Father**, which art in heaven, hallowed be thy name..."*

Matthew 6:9

The relationship between Jesus the Son and God the Father is exhibited on the Cross. We see Jesus addressing God as the Father:

*"**Father**, forgive them; for they know not what they do."*

Luke 23:34

*"**Father**, into thy hands I commend my spirit."*   Luke 23:46

47

The New Testament is full of references to God as the Father of all believers.

> *"Behold, what manner of love the **Father** hath bestowed upon us, that we should be called the sons of God... Behold, now are we the sons of God."*
>
> 1 John 3: 1 & 2

The Son

Islam cannot accept the role of Jesus as the Son of God.

> *"O People of the book! Commit no excess in your religion: nor say of Allah aught but the truth, Christ Jesus the son of Mary was (no more than) a messenger of Allah and His Word, which He bestowed on Mary, and a spirit proceeding from Him. So believe in Allah and His Messenger. Say not **'Trinity'**: desist! It will be better for you. For Allah is One Allah. Glory be to Him: **(Far exalted is He) above having a son."***
>
> Surah 4:171

Nor does Islam accept the deity of Jesus

> **"In blasphemy indeed are those that say that Allah is Christ the son of Mary.** *Say: who then hath the least power against Allah if His will were to destroy Christ the son of Mary, his mother, and all - everyone that is on earth? For to Allah belongeth the dominion of the heavens and the earth, and all that is in between. For Allah hath power over all things."*
>
> Surah 5:17

The God of Islam possesses all power over all things, including the power to erase sin if He so desires and when He so desires. This is completely different from the God of Christianity who is just and merciful, and who must work within the plan of salvation, to satisfy both His mercy and justice. The plan cannot be carried out without the sacrifice of Jesus, the Son of God, on the cross, on our behalf, in order to pay the penalty of our transgression.

> *"For God so loved the world that He gave **His only begotten Son**, that whosoever believeth in Him should not perish, but have everlasting life."*
>
> John 3:16

The love of God towards sinners is against the spirit of Islam. Islam vehemently rejects the crucifixion of Jesus.

> *"That they said (in boast), 'We killed Christ Jesus, the Son of Mary',,,but **they killed him not, nor crucified him**."*
>
> Surah 4:157

The Holy Spirit

Islam looks upon the Holy Spirit as a created spirit the same as an angel. In many instances the Quran uses the name "Holy Spirit" to mean an angel. In the story of the birth of Jesus, the Quran states that God has sent to Mary ***"His Spirit"*** (meaning the Angel Gabriel) to announce to her the news that she was chosen to be the mother of Jesus.

> *"Then We (God) sent to her **Our Angel** (in the original: Our spirit), and he appeared before her as a man in all respects."*
>
> Surah 19:17

The Spirit of God (as the Angel Gabriel) was also the one who allegedly carried the message of the Quran to Mohammed.

> *"Say the **Holy Spirit (The Angel Gabriel)** has brought the revelation from thy Lord in truth."*   Surah 16:102

Because Muslims do not recognize the Holy Spirit, they cannot accept the Lordship of Jesus.

> *"No man can say that Jesus is the Lord, **but by the Holy Ghost**."*   1 Corinthians 12:3

And because Muslims don't have the Holy Spirit dwelling in them, they don't have the assurance of salvation.

> *"The Spirit itself beareth **witness** with our spirit, that we are the **children** of God, and if children, then heirs; heirs of God, and joint heirs with Christ."*   Romans 8:16 & 17

THE "ALLAH" OF ISLAM

In theory Allah in the Quran has 99 names or attributes such as: Omniscient, Omnipotent, Sublime, Living, Everlasting, Holy, Light, Creator, Powerful...etc. In reality, however, the Quran paints a picture of Allah that in many ways resembles

Mohammed's own personality. Somebody suggested that Mohammed, in the Quran, was in fact, *creating a god in his (Mohammed's) own image.*

Whatever Mohammed wanted, Allah wanted for him. However Mohammed reacted, Allah reacted for him. Aisha, (one of Mohammed's 13 wives) was quoted as saying to Mohammed scornfully:

> *"O Allah's Apostle, I do not see but that your Lord hurries in **pleasing** you."*　　　　　　　Al-Bukhari Vol. 7:48

Here are just a few examples:

* When Abu Lahab criticized Mohammed, telling him, "Perish you, Mohammed! Did you invite us here for this?", Allah immediately sends down Surah 111 to condemn both Abu Lahab and his wife.

> ***"Perish the hands of the Father of flame (Abu Lahab).*** *Burnt soon will he be in a fire of blazing flame. His wife shall carry the wood as fuel."*

* When Al Walid Ibn Almoghira and Omaya Ibn Khalaf mocked Mohammed and boasted of their wealth, Allah sends down Surah 104 rebuking them.

> *"Woe to every (kind of) scandal-monger and backbiter who **pileth up wealth** and layeth it by, thinking that wealth would make last forever. He will be sure to be thrown into the fire (of the wrath) of Allah kindled (to a blaze)."*

* When Mohammed fell in love with Zaynab, wife of his adopted son (Zaid), God approved of divorcing her from Zaid and joined her in marriage to Mohammed:

> *"Then, when Zaid had dissolved (his marriage) with her We joined her in marriage to thee, in order that there may be no difficulty to the believers in marriage with the wives of their adopted sons."*　　　　　　　Surah 33:37

- When Mohammed's wives demanded higher allowances out of the booty taken from the massacred Banu Qorayza Jewish tribe, God settled it by telling the wives to either be content with their present allowance or face divorce.

  (See Surah 33:28 & 29)

- When Hafsa caught Mohammed, in her bed, making love to his concubine Mariya, Mohammed tried to please angry Hafsa by promising her that he will stay away from Mariya. At this point Allah intervenes in Mohammed's behalf:

  *"O Prophet why holdest thou to be forbidden that which **Allah has made lawful to thee?** Thou seekest to please thy consorts. But Allah is oft-forgiving, most merciful."*

  Surah 66:1

The list goes on and on. Allah conveniently intervenes to satisfy Mohammed's sexual desires, to support Mohammed's opinions, to justify Mohammed's actions, and to take Mohammed's side whenever he is in trouble.

****

The next time you attend one of those "bridge-building" meetings, where a panel of a Catholic priest, a Protestant minister, a Jewish rabbi and a Muslim sheik, hold hands in solidarity declaring that they all worship the same God, remember these differences!

That bridge they are building is a one way bridge, leading <u>only</u> towards Islam.

4 -JESUS VS. MOHAMMED
What the Bible Teaches About Jesus
What the Quran Teaches About Mohammed

* ### JESUS IS THE SON OF GOD
"Say ye of him, whom the Father hath sanctified, and sent to the world, thou blasphemest, because I said, I am the Son of God?" John 10:36

MOHAMMED WAS A MAN
"I am but a man like yourselves." Surah 18:110

* ### JESUS PERFORMED MIRACLES
"He (Jesus) hath done all things well: he maketh both the deaf to hear, and the dumb to speak." Mark 7:37

MOHAMMED DID NOT
"And we refrain from sending the signs, only because the men of former generations treated them as false." Surah 17:59

* ### JESUS KNEW WHAT IS INSIDE PEOPLE'S HEARTS
"And all the churches shall know that I am He which searcheth the reins and hearts." Revelation 2:23

MOHAMMED DID NOT
"I tell you not that with me are the treasures of Allah. , nor do I know what is hidden. Nor claim I to be an angel."
Surah 11:31

* ### JESUS IS OUR ADVOCATE WITH GOD THE FATHER
"If any man sin, we have an advocate with the Father, Jesus Christ the righteous: and He is the propitiation for our sins: and not for ours only, but also for the sins of the whole world."
1 John 2:1 & 2

MOHAMMED WAS NOT

"Whether thou ask for their forgiveness or not, if you ask seventy times for their forgiveness, Allah will not forgive them."   Surah 9:80

* JESUS FORBADE HIS FOLLOWERS FROM USING THE SWORD

"Put up again thy sword into his place: for all they that take the sword shall perish with the sword."   Matthew 26:52

MOHAMMED URGED HIS FOLLOWERS TO USE THE SWORD

"O Prophet! Rouse the believers to the fight."   Surah 8:65

* JESUS TAUGHT FORGIVENESS

"Ye have heard that it hath been said, An eye for an eye, and a tooth for a tooth. But I say unto you that ye resist not evil: but whosoever shall smite thee on thy right cheek, turn to him the other also."   Matthew 5:38, 39

MOHAMMED TAUGHT REVENGE

"If then anyone transgress the prohibition against you, transgress ye likewise against him."   Surah 2:194

* JESUS WAS SINLESS

"Who did no sin, neither was guile found in his mouth."
                                      1 Peter 2:22

MOHAMMED WAS SINFUL

"Ask forgiveness for thy fault, and for the men and women who believe."   Surah 47:19

* JESUS' WORDS NEVER CHANGED

"Heaven and earth shall pass away, but my words shall not pass away."   Matthew 24:35

THE QURAN'S WORDS CHANGED

"When we substitute one revelation for another - and Allah

knows best what he reveals." Surah 16:101

* JESUS CAST SATAN AWAY
"Then saith Jesus unto him, Get thee hence, Satan."
Matthew 4:10

MOHAMMED ASSOCIATED WITH DEMONS
"Behold, we turned towards thee a company of Jinns (demons), listening to the Quran; when they stood in the presence thereof, they said, 'Listen in silence.' When the (reading) was finished, they returned to their people, to warn them." Surah 46:29

* SATAN HAD NO INFLUENCE OVER JESUS
"The prince of this world (Satan) cometh, and has nothing in me." John 14:30

SATAN HAD INFLUENCE OVER MOHAMMED
"If a suggestion from Satan assails thy (mind), seek refuge with Allah; for He heareth and knoweth (all things)." Surah 7:200
(See also Surah 113: 4)

* JESUS HEALED THE BLIND MAN
"As he was come nigh unto Jericho, a certain blind man sat by the wayside begging.
And hearing the multitude pass by, he asked what it meant.
And they told him, that Jesus of Nazareth passeth by.
And he cried, saying, Jesus, thou son of David, have mercy on me.
And they which went before rebuked him, that he should hold his peace: but he cried so much the more, Thou son of David have mercy on me. And Jesus stood, and commanded him to be brought unto him; and when he was come near, he asked him, saying, what wilt thou that I shall do unto thee? And he said, Lord, that I may receive my sight.
And Jesus said unto him, receive thy sight; thy faith hath saved thee. And immediately he received his sight, and followed him, glorifying God." Luke 18:35-43

MOHAMMED TURNED AWAY FROM THE BLIND MAN

"(Mohammed) frowned and turned away because there came to him the blind man. But what could tell thee but that perchance he might grow (in spiritual understanding). Or that he might receive admonition, and the teaching might profit him?

As to one who regards himself as self-sufficient, to him dost thou attend; Though it is no blame to thee if he grow not (in spiritual understanding). But as to him who came to thee striving earnestly, and with fear (in his heart), of him was thou unmindful." Surah 80:1-10

* JESUS CALLED ON PEOPLE TO COME TO HIM

"Come unto me, all ye that labour and are heavily laden, and I will give you rest. Take my yoke upon you, and learn of me; for I am meek and lowly in heart: and ye shall find rest unto your souls. For my yoke is easy, and my burden is light."

Matthew 11:28-30

MOHAMMED WAS ADMONISHED BECAUSE HE SENT PEOPLE AWAY

"Send not away those who call on their Lord morning and evening seeking His face. In naught art thou accountable for them, and in naught are they accountable for thee, that thou shouldst turn them away, and thus be (one) of the unjust."

Surah 6:52

* JESUS TAUGHT MONOGAMY

"For this cause shall a man leave father and mother, and shall cleave to his wife; and they twain shall be one flesh, wherefore they are no more twain, but one flesh. What therefore God has joined together, let not man part asunder." Matthew 19:5&6

MOHAMMED TAUGHT POLYGAMY

"If ye fear that ye shall not be able to deal justly with the orphans, marry women of your choice two, or three, or four. But if ye fear that ye shall not be able to deal justly (with them) then only one." Surah 4:3

* ## JESUS CAME TO SAVE LIVES

"For the Son of man is not come to destroy men's lives, but to save them." Luke 9:56

MOHAMMED WAS CALLED TO DESTROY LIVES

"Say to the desert Arabs who lagged behind: Ye shall be summoned (to fight) against a people given to vehement war: then shall ye fight, or they shall submit. Then if ye show obedience, Allah will grant ye a goodly reward, but if ye turn back as ye did before, He will punish you with a grievous penalty." Surah 48:16

* ## PEOPLE WERE FREE TO ACCEPT JESUS' MESSAGE, OR REJECT IT

"But into whatsoever city you enter, and they receive you not, go your ways out into the streets of the same, and say, Even the very dust of your city, which cleaveth on us, we do wipe off against you: notwithstanding be ye sure of this, that the kingdom of God is come nigh unto you." Luke 10:10, 11

PEOPLE WERE FORCED TO ACCEPT MOHAMMED'S MESSAGE

"Fight those who believe not in Allah nor the last day...Nor acknowledge the religion of truth (Islam), (even if they are) of the people of the Book, until they pay the Jizya (tribute tax) with willing submission, and feel themselves subdued."

Surah 9:29

* ## JESUS IS THE LIFE, AND HIS FOLLOWERS WILL LIVE

"I am the resurrection, and the life: he that believeth in me, though he were dead, yet shall he live." John 11:25

MOHAMMED DIED, AND HIS FOLLOWERS WILL ALSO DIE

"Truly thou wilt die, and truly they (too) will die."

Surah 39:30

5 - JESUS IS THE DIFFERENCE

Jesus Christ cannot be described as just another good messenger of God. Jesus was different from all other human beings of any time and place, *and He makes the difference.*

By His words, Jesus set the perfect example.
Nobody ever spoke as He did. His teachings expressed the perfect example in ethics, conduct, and worship (See Matthew 5-7). *Christianity, however, is more than just a set of noble teachings.*

By His life, Jesus was the perfect example.
Jesus was the only one, ever, who could declare that He was without sin (John 8:46). His claim was confirmed by friends and foes alike (Luke 23:14; Matthew 27:4; Matthew 27:24; Luke 23:47). Jesus lived every word that He spoke. *Yet no man, on his own, can perfectly follow Jesus' example.*

By His power, Jesus enables us to follow his example.
Jesus doesn't simply order us to do good; rather, *He changes our hearts so that we love doing good.*

A miracle is performed in every person who puts his trust in the perfection of Christ. Through faith in Christ, we can be spiritually "born again" into the family of God. This miracle has happened in the lives of millions throughout history, whom God has changed from hopeless sinners to beloved sons, by the power and work of His Holy Spirit.

Chapter V
IS ISLAM A LEGITIMATE EXTENSION OF CHRISTIANITY?

Islam in the West is fighting a battle for acceptance and legitimacy. Muslim activists are waging a fierce campaign trying to convince Christians and Jews that Islam is a "heavenly" religion. They stress that Islam believes in Moses and Jesus, that Mohammed is a continuation and culmination of the prophets, and that Mohammed is the seal of all prophets. They even claim that Mohammed was prophesied in the Bible.

1 - WAS MOHAMMED PROPHESIED IN THE BIBLE?

Muslims cite many references in both Old and New Testaments to prove that Mohammed was prophesied in the Bible. However, a close examination of these references reveals that they don't fit Mohammed. These are references that usually point either to Jesus or the Holy Spirit. Here are the frequently quoted examples:

In the Old Testament: *"The Lord thy God will raise up unto thee a prophet from the midst of thee, of thy brethren, like unto me; unto him ye shall hearken. I will raise them up a prophet from among their brethren, like unto thee, and will put my words in his mouth; and he shall speak unto them all that I shall command him."*

(Deuteronomy 18:15 & 18)

This can't possibly refer to Mohammed. Mohammed is the descendant of Ishmael, and the Jews never looked at the descendants of Ishmael as "brothers." On the other hand Jesus fits the description "like unto Moses." Jesus was a Hebrew, as was Moses, while Mohammed was not. Jesus performed signs and wonders, as did Moses, and Mohammed did not. Peter, in the New Testament, left no doubt about the fact that this prophecy applies to Jesus. (See Acts 3:20-26)

In the New Testament: *"But when the Comforter is come, whom I will send unto you from the Father, even the Spirit of truth, which proceedeth from the Father, he shall testify of me."* (John 15:26)

Muslims assert that the Greek word which was translated *"the comforter"*, actually means *"the praised one"* or *"Mahmoud"* in Arabic, in reference to Mohammed. While it is true that there is a word, similar in pronunciation, which means *"the praised one,"* however the word used in the Gospels is different and is accurately translated to *"the Comforter."* This, no doubt, refers to the Holy Spirit. The Holy Spirit is a spirit, while Mohammed was flesh. The Holy Spirit was sent to the disciples, but Mohammed came 6 centuries after the death of the disciples. It was said that The Holy Spirit would "dwell" with the disciples (John14:16). On the other hand Mohammed never saw the disciples. It was said that the world would "not see" the Holy Spirit, but people saw Mohammed.

2 - DO ISLAM AND CHRISTIANITY AGREE ON THE BASICS?

Muslim activists in the West are using another tactic to create an atmosphere of acceptance. They stress that *Islam and Christianity have a lot in common*. They cite Islam's belief in the Bible, God, Jesus, the Virgin Mary, the prophets, the Day of Judgment and Paradise.

The fact is that the differences between Christianity and Islam are very deep, and irreconcilable. The space limitation will enable us to list just a few.

God of the Bible is not *Allah of the Quran*

God of the Bible is a loving Father, who along with the Son and the Holy Spirit, is One God.
* **To Muslims, the concept of a triune God is a blasphemy.**
  *"They do **blaspheme** who say Allah is **one of three...**, for there is no God except one Allah."* Surah 5:73

- **Allah of Islam is changeable.**
  "None of our revelations do we abrogate or cause to be forgotten, but we substitute (with) something better or similar. Knowest thou not that Allah hath power over all things."
  Surah 2:106
- **Allah of Islam is temperamental.**
  "If we had so willed, we could certainly have brought every soul its true guidance, but the word from me will come true "I will fill Hell with Jinns (demons) and men all together."
  Surah 32:13
- **Allah of Islam is a deceiver.**
  "They plot and plan, and Allah, too plans, but the best of planners (deceivers) is Allah."   Surah 8:30
- **Allah of Islam is frightening.**
  *"It is Allah whom ye should more justly **fear**, if you believe."*
  Surah 9:13

Jesus of the Bible is not *Isa of the Quran*

Jesus of the Bible is the Son of God who died on the Cross to save the whole world. In the Quran Jesus' name is Isa.
- **Isa is a created human being.**
  *"The similitude of Isa before Allah is as that of Adam; **He created him from dust,** Then said to him: "Be": and he was."*
  Surah 3:59
- **Isa is just a prophet.**
  *"O people of the book (Christians) commit no excess in your religion: nor say of Allah aught but truth, Christ Isa the son of Mary was (No more than) a **messenger** of Allah."*
  Surah 4:171
- **Isa was not crucified.**
  *"That they said (in boast) "we killed Christ Isa, the son of Mary"...but they **killed him not**, nor crucified him."*
  Surah 4:157
- **Isa will return to earth to destroy the Cross.**
  *"The hour will not be established until the son of Mary (Jesus) descends amongst you as a just ruler, **he will break the Cross..**"*
  Hadith vol. 3:656

The Holy Spirit of the Bible is not Angel Gabriel of the Quran

The Holy Spirit in the Bible is the third person in the Godhead. His work is to comfort, convict, regenerate, guide, give power and bring forth fruit.

- **The Holy Spirit in Islam is an angel.**

  *"Then we (Allah) sent to her (Mary) our **Angel** (our spirit), and he (Angel Gabriel) appeared before her as a man in all respects."* Surah 19:17

  *"Say the **Holy Spirit** (the Angel Gabriel) has brought the revelation (the Quran) from thy Lord in Truth."* Surah 16:102

Ethics of the Bible are not Sharia of the Quran

Ethics of the Bible are based on love, forgiveness, equality, tolerance and free-choice.

- **Islam teaches revenge.**

  *"If any one transgresses the prohibition against you, **transgress likewise against him.**"* Surah 2:194

- **Islam does not treat women and men as equal.**

  *"..to the male a portion equal to that of **two** females."*
  Surah 4:11

- **Islam allows men to beat their wives.**

  *"... As to those women on whose part ye fear disloyalty and ill-conduct, **admonish them, refuse to share their beds, beat them.**"*
  Surah 4:34

- **Islam imposes harsh physical punishment on wrongdoers.**

  *A thief is punished by the amputation of hands. Surah 5:38
  *A drunk is punished by 80 lashes. Hadith vol. 8:770
  *An adulterer is punished by 100 lashes. Surah 24:2

- **Islam must be imposed by force, if necessary.**

  *"And **fight** them on, until there is no more tumult (seduction) or oppression, and there prevail justice, and faith in Allah (**and the religion becomes that of Allah**)."* Surah 2:193

- **Apostasy from Islam is punishable by death.**

  *"Whoever changes his (Islamic) religion, **kill him.**"*
  Hadith vol. 9:57

Salvation of the Bible is not *the straight path of the Quran*

Salvation in the Bible is guaranteed by the redemptive work of Jesus Christ on our behalf, on the Cross.

- **In Islam, there is no Original Sin, and no need for the Cross; Allah, the all powerful, has the supreme authority to punish or to forgive whomever He pleaseth, whenever He pleaseth.**

    *"He (Allah) forgiveth whom He pleaseth, and punisheth whom He pleaseth,... for **Allah has power over all things**."*

    Surah 2:284

- **In Islam, good deeds cancel bad deeds.**

    "For those things that are good remove those that are evil."

    Surah 11:114

- **The only assurance a Muslim has of going to Paradise is through fighting for the cause of spreading Islam (Jihad), and being martyred in the process.**

    *"And if you are slain, or die in the way of Allah, **forgiveness** and mercy from Allah are far better than all they could amass."*

    Surah 3:157

Heaven of the Bible is not *Paradise of the Quran*

Heaven's pleasures in the Bible are pleasures of spirit, pleasures of purity.

- **In Islam Paradise is the place where a Muslim man will be reclining, eating meats and delicious fruits, drinking exquisite wines, and engaging in sex with beautiful women** (and perpetually young beautiful boys *"Wildan or Ghilman"*, according to some Muslim theologians).

    *"As to the righteous, they will be in gardens and in happiness (to them will be said:) "Eat and **drink** ye, with profit and health, because of your (good) deeds "They will **recline** (with ease) on thrones (of dignity) arranged in ranks; and we shall **join (marry) them** to companions with beautiful big and*

*lustrous eyes... And we shall bestow on them, of **fruit and meat,** anything they desire. They shall there exchange, one another, **a cup** free of frivolity, free of all taint of ill. Round about them will serve to them, **young male servants** as pearls well-guarded."*   Surah 52:17, 19, 20 & 22-24

Dear Christian Brother/Sister

The present trend, among well-meaning Christians, calls for understanding, making dialogue and building bridges between Christianity and Islam. These words sound good, but unfortunately, the manner in which they are applied often reflects naiveté.

True understanding occurs when we try to know both the attractive side of Islam and the ugly side. True dialogue occurs when we listen to them and we insist they listen to us. True bridge building occurs when the bridges we build with them go both ways. True love occurs when we tell them they are wrong if we know that they are wrong.

The current Muslims' message to Christians in the West, "We have lots in common with you, we are similar, accept us, listen to us..." It is a ploy, don't believe it, as it is designed solely to spread their religion. After they gain the upper hand, Muslims' message will be, "We have nothing in common with you, you are infidels who worship three gods, and follow a corrupt Bible. You are *dhimmis* who must accept Islam or pay *jizya* (penalty tax) for being Christians..." Then, there would be no understanding between Muslims and Christians, no dialogues, and no bridges....

Don't believe the Muslims' deception that Islam is a legitimate extension of Christianity. The Bible makes it clear that, *"last of all,"* God the Father sent His Son Jesus (Matthew 21:37), and that the Bible is God's last revelation (Revelation 22:18). Jesus warns, "There shall arise false prophets, that if it were possible, they shall deceive the very elect."   Matthew 24:24

CONCLUSION

And, now, there is a question to be asked:

WHAT DO YOU **THINK OF** JESUS CHRIST?

The Quran views Jesus as simply a prophet, a good man, who performed some miracles. The Quran denies His crucifixion; it is too degrading, and cannot accept His Lordship; it is too exalting. Yet, in order to save us from sin, Jesus of the Bible was both. **He lowered Himself to where sin had brought us, and redeemed us on the cross. Then He lifted us to heaven, and reconciled us with God the Father.**

From the beginning, God had a plan for the eternal salvation of mankind. This plan is non-negotiable and non-changeable. After Adam and Eve fell into sin, God provided that the seed of the woman (Jesus) shall bruise the serpent's (Satan's) head, and that the serpent will bruise His heel (Genesis 3:15). Throughout the Old Testament, God was dealing with His people through sacrifices that pointed to the ultimate coming sacrifice of Jesus Christ. After Jesus was born, John the Baptist declared that Jesus was "the Lamb of God, which taketh away the sin of the world." John 1:29. This declaration and all the promises of the Old Testament were fulfilled when Jesus Christ died on the cross on our behalf, obtaining eternal redemption and salvation for all mankind.

Nobody other than Jesus ever claimed that he could forgive sin and give the assurance of salvation from sin. The Bible says: "Neither is there salvation in any (person) other (than Jesus): for there is none other name under heaven given among men, whereby we must be saved." Acts 4:12

And, there is a decision to be made:

WHAT WILL YOU **DO WITH** JESUS CHRIST?

Whether you accept Him, reject Him, or simply do nothing, **you will be making a decision.**

While "Allah" in the Quran commands Muslims to "fight the unbelievers," The God of the Bible does not force anyone to choose Him, neither will His people fight to force others. It is each person's free choice to accept or reject Jesus Christ as Lord and Savior.

My prayer is that your decision will be to accept Him today.

"Believe in the Lord Jesus, and you will be saved."   Acts 16:31

Dear God,
I acknowledge that I can never, on my own, live up to your standards. I believe that Jesus died for me to pay the penalty of my sinfulness and rose again to give me a new life. I ask that you forgive me, and give me a new heart and a whole new life that will follow Jesus' example. In the name of Jesus Christ my Lord I pray,
                                                                Amen

KNOW THE TRUTH
FOLLOW THE TRUTH
SPREAD THE TRUTH

"You shall know the truth, and the truth shall make you free." (John 8:32)

ISLAM UNVEILED

is now available in English, Arabic, French, Spanish, German and Dutch.

THE ISLAMIZATION OF AMERICA

The Islamic Strategies and the Christian Response

A new book by Abdullah Al-Araby. It reflects the cry of Abdullah's heart to offer America an eye-opening wake-up call. It is far more than just another book on Islam. It unveils the Islamic strategies used to Islamize America. It offers a practical plan to stop the obliteration of our Christian civilization before it is too late.

LIST OF AVAILABLE TRACTS

- Islam; the facade, the facts
- The <u>real</u> attitude of Islam towards Christians and Jews.
- Save America
- If Islam ruled America
- Neither Black nor African
- Being a Muslim's wife
- To kill and to die IN THE NAME OF ALLAH
- Islam; What Muslims don't tell you
- Nothing in Common
- The Concept of Sin in Islam

THE PEN vs. THE SWORD

is a volunteer-run, interdenominational Christian ministry, committed to revealing the truth about Islam. Many of our publications are distributed free of charge to all continents of the world. All revenues go to the actual cost of producing and shipping the materials. We invite you to take part in this ministry. Your contribution is needed, and very much appreciated.

VISIT US ON THE WEB
http://www.IslamReview.com
E-Mail: TheTruth@aol.com